Say it in Scots

WHA'S LIKE US?

Say it in Scots

WHA'S
LIKE US?

Chris Robinson

BLACK & WHITE PUBLISHING

First published 2008
by Black & White Publishing Ltd
99 Giles Street, Edinburgh EH6 6BZ

ISBN: 978 1 84502 197 9

1 3 5 7 9 10 8 6 4 2   08 09 10 11 12

Copyright © Chris Robinson, 2008
Illustrations by Garry Thorburn
www.caricaturecards.co.uk

Typeset by Ellipsis Books Ltd
Printed and bound by Nørhaven Paperback A/S

Contents

Say it in Scots

Whether you are a Scots speaker already, or whether you are a visitor to Scotland, this series of books is guaranteed to awaken your enthusiasm for the Scots language. There is bound to be something in these books to interest you. They are based on the *Scottish National Dictionary* and *A Dictionary of the Older Scottish Tongue*, which are now available online as the *Dictionary of the Scots Language* at **www.dsl.ac.uk.** Additional material comes from the ongoing research of Scottish Language Dictionaries, who are responsible for the stewardship of these great reference works and for keeping the record of Scots words up to date.

Scots is the language of Lowland Scotland and the Northern Isles. It is also used in parts of Ulster. Along with English and Gaelic, it is one of Scotland's three indigenous languages.

Scots is descended from Northern Old English, itself greatly influenced by Old Scandinavian. From the twelfth century onwards, it became increasingly established in Lowland Scotland and was then enriched by words borrowed from French, Latin, Gaelic and Dutch. It was the language of government, spoken by kings, courtiers, poets and the people. It has a literary heritage the equal of any in Europe.

Like any other language, it has its own dialects such as Glaswegian, Ayrshire, Shetland, Doric, Border Scots and many others. These have a rich diversity and share a central core uniting them as varieties of the Scots language. We have tried to reflect the history and variety of Scots in these books and hope you will find some words that you can savour on your tongue and slip into everyday conversation.

Some of the spelling, especially in the older quotations, may be unfamiliar, but if you try reading the quotations out loud, you'll find they aren't difficult to understand.

Chris Robinson

Director

Scottish Language Dictionaries

www.scotsdictionaries.org.uk

Introduction

O wad some pooer the giftie gie us
Tae see oorsels as ithers see us.

(ROBERT BURNS)

When someone says 'Scotsman' or 'Scotswoman' to
you, what kind of person immediately springs to mind?
Is it the tartan-clad Highlander saying 'Hoots mon, och
aye the noo?' Or is it the character of Rab C. Nesbitt? Or
is it the neat, friendly, shortbread-baking grannie? Are
the Scots really mean? Or is Scottish hospitality second
to none? Are we a race of drunks or a race of puritans?
Many nationalities have been subjected to stereotyping
and the Scots are no exception. What this book aims
to do is explode some of the myths and peer into the
private lives of the Scots, examining the deepest recesses
of their psyches. I can't promise *see oorsels as ithers see*

us, but the words we use to describe ourselves are very revealing.

However, trying to *see* ourselves through the words we use comes with a built-in difficulty: there are far more words in Scots for criticising than for praising! If we *gie someone their character*, it will be an honest appraisal, and we are not given to flattery. William Dunbar has used more disparaging words than most in his virtuoso poetry, most famously in *The Flyting of Dunbar and Kennedy* – a contest in insults between two very skilful poets. However, it is another of Dunbar's poems that I will take as a starting point for this book, *The Dance of the Sevin Deidly Synnis*. What are the sins that Scots have been guilty of, and what are our redeeming virtues?

Many of the words we know and use today in Scots can be traced back through the centuries and, if they are as current now as they were in the long-distant past, has the Scottish character really changed all that much? Let's see if we can really uncover something of the true Scottish character and find out Wha's Like Us?

1 Pride

And first of all in dance wes Pryd
With hair wyld back and bonet on syde.

(WILLIAM DUNBAR)

"Yon is pride," said Mungo the priest, "and it is one
of the seven woesome sins which make a devil's
kingrik of this world."

(COLIN MACKAY *The Song of the Forest* 1986)

If there is one sin that the Scots dislike in other people, it is the sin of pride. At the first sign of anyone getting a bit above himself or herself, a fellow Scot will be ready with an appropriate put-down. As soon as someone gets on in the world and gives themselves airs and graces, a detractor will remark "Jist wha daes he think he is?" The most famous Scots response to those who would set a high value on themselves is the great Burns poem, *A Man's a Man for A' That*:

The honest man, tho' e'er sae poor,
Is king o'men for a' that.

Nevertheless, pride still lurks in the mountains and valleys of Scotland and several authorities, like Dunbar, acknowledge it to be the first of the deadly sins. One such authority is John Barbour in his *Legends of the Saints* (1380):

Of synnis kyndis are thre, & the formaste pride
ma be.

And, according to Johannes de Irland in *The Meroure of Wyssdome* (1490),

> *the prince of prid, lord of all iniquite and myrknes is Lucifer himself.*

So pride, manifested in 'self-esteem, arrogance, conceit, presumption; vanity, the outward appearance of pride, pomp, splendour, ostentation', as the *Dictionary of the Scots Language* defines it, is a bad thing, but those Scots who have in the past pursued the paths of wickedness have left us many words for pride.

So let's have a look at some proud words and modest words to help us start finding out what the Scots *really* think about themselves.

Antisyzygy – (pronounced antie-zizzidgy) the poet Hugh MacDiarmid wrote of the Caledonian Antisyzygy as the opposing forces in the Scottish psyche which contribute to its genius. The *Sunday Herald* (19 December 1999) referred to it with equal accuracy as *our national brand of cultural schizophrenia.*

Bigsy – conceited. Scots are often sparing with praise in case people get bigsy, but some there are some characters for whom being bigsy is part of their nature. The frog in John Caie's poem was one such – and he came to a bad end:

> The bigsy wee cratur was feelin that prood,
>> He gapit his mou an he croakit oot lood:
>> "Gin ye'd a' like tae see a richt puddock,"
>> quo he,
>> "Ye'll never, I'll sweer, get a better nor me."

Birkie – a conceited man. Robert Burns was quick to pounce on anyone showing an excess of pride:

> Ye see yon birkie ca'd a lord
> Wha struts an' stares an' a' that
> Tho' hundreds worship at his word
> He's but a coof for a' that.

Brank – bear oneself proudly, strut.

Cockapentie – a snob.
> *He's a richt wee cockapentie. Ye wad think he wis*
> *Lord Muck o Stoorie Castle.*

Consait – *tae hae a guid consait o yersel* is to have a
good opinion of yourself.

Crouse – (pronounced croose) proud.
> *She's fair crouse in her braw wee hoose.*

Dink – haughty.
> *See her lookin sae dink wi her neb [nose] in the air.*

Hautane – haughty. Andrew of Winton in *The
Orygynale Cronykil of* Scotland (c.1420) noted that the
clergy were not above sin:
> *Byschapys, prestys, and prelatys In hawtayne pryd*
> *ay led thair statys.*

Orgueille – to quote Gilbert Hay:
> *that is callit pryde, thinkis na man pere till him*

[thinks no man his equal]
and is a grete vice.

(*The Buke of Knychthede* 1456)

Orguillouse – proud. This was a favourite word of Gilbert Hay, whose *Buke of the Law of Armys* (1456) laments that

Thare is sum men sa hichty, hautayn, and orguillous and full of surquedry.

However, he assures us that they are not in line for promotion because:

na orguillouse squyer suld nocht enter in knychthede.

Pauchtie – supercilious.

Pride in outward appearance – is recognised by Alexander Arbuthnot (c.1585):

Coistlie claythis . . . Quhilk dois bot foster pryide and vanitie.

Also, from the *Bannatyne Manuscript*, we learn that
*Pryd is amangis ws enterit . . . And lerd our lordis to
go . . . With silkin gownis*

[Pride has entered among us and taught our lords
to go with silken gowns].

On the other hand, James Kelly in his 1721 collection
of proverbs warns against a kind of inverted sartorial
snobbery:
Honesty is no Pride.

This is directed towards people who make a point of
dressing carelessly. He would not have approved of
grunge.

Pridefu – full of pride.

Pride-prankit – puffed up with pride, self-assured,
arrogant.

Puft up – puffed up. The alliteration has proved irresistible to writers over the centuries and so we find many characters puft up with pride, or even, through personification, used of Pride itself:

> *Fy, puft vp pryde, thow is full poysonabill*
>
> (ROBERT HENRYSON *Fables* c.1500)

The clergy seem to have had a particular propensity for being puft with pride and so Quintin Kennedy writes in Ane litil breif tracteit..prevand the real body of *Jesu Crist* to be present in the sacrament (c.1561) of

> *The pestilent preacheouris puft vp with vayne glore.*

Puftly – This succinct adverb, formed from puft, appears in

> *Or yit so puftlye lift thair headis in vanetie and pryde*

(*The Works of William Fowler, Secretary to Queen Anne* c.1590
ed. W. FOWLER, H. W. MEIKLE, J. CRAIGIE, and J. PURVES)

Scabbert – aspiring to gentility.

Scottish Cringe – Billy Kay, the author, broadcaster, authority on Scots and energetic advocate for the language, writes:

> . . . as most MSPs and most Scots have not been educated in their own culture, ignorant attitudes abound, and the Scottish Cringe is everywhere. I collect examples: the education convener in a Labour fiefdom who replied to the proposal that Scottish studies should be an integral part of his schools' curriculum, "Oh, no, we live in a multi-cultural environment!" Apparently every culture was to be taught except the native one!
>
> A few years ago when I asked a Fife headmaster if Scottish literature was encouraged in his school, the reply left me almost speechless . . . "No, this is not a very Scottish area." Can you imagine an English or Irish headmaster making such a statement?
>
> It shows how far we have to go in renewing

Scotland after centuries of self inflicted cultural colonialism. I have actually heard educated Scots argue that no Scottish history from before 1707 should be taught in our schools, as it only foments 'dangerous nationalism'. The Catalans reckoned it would take three generations after autonomy for a similar 'slave mentality' to be replaced with cultural and political self confidence. With us it might take a bittie longer!

Many Scots deny the existence of the Cringe but very few wholeheartedly embrace what has been called the 'shortbread tin' image of Scottish culture. Fortunately we have a new wave of writers and musicians who are powering Scottish culture to undreamt-of heights and our young people have a new self-confidence and an international outlook.

Sneist – behave in an arrogant way.

Succudry, Surquedry – overweening pride, arrogance, presumptuousness.

It is surquidy, gif a capitane, with L. [50] *men of*
armes, wald assailye thre hundreth als gude; that
war fule hardynes, and na vertu morale

(GILBERT HAY The Buke of the Law of Arms 1456)

Superciliosity – pride. William Birnie's edifying
work, recommending decorous and modest interment,
The Blame of Kirk-buriall tending to perswade Cemiteriall
Civilitie (1606), highlights the victory of death over pride:

For many to eternize their soone forgot memory . . .
hes prepared pyramides of pomp, others pillers of
pride . . . As if such superciliosity could sweeten the
bitter swarfes of their sowre death.

Proverbs and sayings

The most famous proverb relating to pride is *Pride goeth*
before a fall, (based on the Old Testament *Book of*
Proverbs 16:18, which, in the King James version, reads:

Pride goeth before destruction, and an haughty
spirit before a fall.

This appears in Scottish literature in the *Book of the Howlat* (c.1450–2) by Sir Richard Holland as

> *Pryde neuer yit left His feir but a fall*

[Pride never yet left his companion without a fall]

and this is very similarly expressed by Stewart in the *Metrical Chronicle of Scotland* (1535) as

> *Pryde left neuir his maist[er] but ane fall.*

The idea that in some way people are misled by pride is expressed in a quotation from *The Buike of King Allexander the Conqueroure*, translated by Sir Gilbert Hay (c.1460):

> *Hichty men that pride dissavis ay.*

A kent his faither – [I knew his father] is the put-down for someone from your community who does well and then puts on airs.

All fur coat and nae knickers – is a saying much used in Edinburgh. It is used of people who put on an outward show. It is alternatively expressed as **pianos and kippers** suggesting the clinging-on to appearances of people in straitened circumstances; they may have a piano in the drawing room but they eat the cheapest of food when unobserved. Formerly, this was sometimes directed at ladies of the middle-class area of Edinburgh known as Morningside, which even had its own genteel accent but, as a result of two world wars and a changing economy, had a high proportion of single or widowed women living on ever more modest incomes. While trying to keep up standards can hardly be classed as a deadly sin, James Carmichael's *Collection of Proverbs* (c.1628) maintains:

It is pride but proffitt to weir gloves and ga barfet.

To set or turn out the brunt [burnt] *side o yer shin* – to be proud of yourself, to hold your head high. Allan Ramsay uses this expression and defends the justifiable pride of poets in their own work in a poem of 1719:

Set out the burnt Side of your Shin, For Pride in Poets is nae Sin.

Why anyone should burn their shins in the first place is not certain.

We wouldn't call the Queen our auntie – we feel equal to royalty; we are as good as anyone. This is illustrated in a poignant reminiscence from The *Herald* (26 January 2000):

> *When I was but a little tiny lad I had, like everyone else in Glasgow, a great civic pride in our water. We may have had more flea bites than freckles, and looked like Mel Gibson in* Braveheart *with blue ointment painted over our impetigo'd faces, but as far as the stuff that came through the lead pipes and out of the one (cold) tap in the house and the cistern of the stairhead privy was concerned, we wouldn't call the Queen our auntie.*

Glasgow's water is supplied from Loch Katrine in the Trossachs, a place of outstanding beauty and pure water. The lead pipes which took it to the kitchen sink have now been replaced.

To put someone's gas at a peep – means to bring someone down a peg.

Here is a translation of the Aesop fable in which pride is mocked:

Maister Corbie on a bough
Hauds a kebbock [cheese] *in his mou.*
Maister Tod [fox], *wha smells the cheese,*
Waftin doucely in the breeze,
Luiks up an says, "My! Whitna craw!
A maun declare, yer unco braw,
An if yer singin's hauf as guid
Ye'll be the toast o a the wuid."
The puft up corbie's affa prood,
Opens his beak and skreechs oot lood.
The kebbock faas; the tod is quick;
Ower late the craw perceives the trick.
The Moral's clear, nae need tae threap [nag, go on*
            and on]
The corbie's gas is at a peep.

Here's tae us. Wha's like us? Damn few an they're a deid – a Scottish toast with a curious combination of pride and pessimism (See **Antisyzygy**). The *Press and Journal* (21 October 2003) asserts:

> *It is insecurity, not arrogance, which breeds aggressive "Wha's like us?" braggadocio. It's lack of confidence which produces the Scottish cringe, as we alternate between national glory and national paranoia. Our fragile football team bears the brunt of inflated expectations and morbid pessimism. This is Hugh MacDiarmid's "Caledonian antisyzygy", or Scottish dualism, in a dark blue jersey.*

The upside of pride

But is pride really such a bad thing? Do we not all have things that we are right to be proud of? The *Dictionary of the Scots Language* gives further meanings of pride as the 'cream', the 'flower', the 'glory', the 'joy' (of a person or group). We can all aspire to greater things and there is no sin in being *sodger-clad but major-mindit*.

Ten things for Scots to be proud of:

1. Scottish literature

From Barbour's *Bruce* (1375) to the appointment of Edinburgh in 2004 as the first City of Literature, Scotland has produced authors of the first rank. As well known as Burns is, he is just one star in a galaxy of Scottish writers in both Scots and English.

2. Scottish music

The fiddle music, bagpipe music and songs of Scotland can make the feet itch to dance or wring the heart. We have a whole new generation of virtuosi performing traditional music and creating a new and exciting heritage for musicians in the years to come.

3. Scottish engineering and science

James Clerk Maxwell (electro-magnetism), Alexander

Graham Bell (telephone) , John Logie Baird (television), Alexander Fleming (penicillin), James Young Simpson (anaesthesia), Joseph Lister (antisepsis), John Napier (logarithms), Thomas Telford (civil engineering, canals, roads, bridges, churches), Robert Stevenson (lighthouses), John Boyd Dunlop (pneumatic tyres), Dugald Clerk (two-stroke engine), James Watt (steam engine), James Black (thermochemistry), James Dewar (thermos flask), Charles Macintosh (raincoats), and James 'Paraffin' Young (extraction of oil from coal and shale) are just a few of the great Scots inventors and researchers.

4. Scottish art and architecture

James Craig, Sir Robert Lorimer, Charles Rennie Mackintosh, James Adam, Robert Adam, William Henry Playfair and Basil Spence are some of the best-known architects from Scotland. Many elegant, practical, defensive or decorative buildings are lasting monuments to the famous and less well-known Scots architects. Artists include Henry Raeburn, Allan Ramsay, Alexander

Naysmith, Samuel John Peploe, Anne Redpath, Elizabeth Blackadder, Joan Eardley, John Byrne (also a playwright) and Jack Vettriano. These are a sample of the artists whose work can be seen in the great galleries in Scotland and throughout the world.

5. Scottish food

Deep-fried Mars Bars aside, Scotland produces fish, meat, fruit and vegetables of the finest quality and now has some of the world's finest chefs and restaurants.

6. Scottish wildlife

A large part of Scotland is sparsely inhabited and offers a safe environment for many birds and animals from the red deer to the gold-crested wren.

7. Scottish adventure

Scotland has sent explorers and missionaries to all parts of the globe. Now we invite visitors to come here and experience the variety of outdoor activities from mountaineering to white-water rafting, ski-ing to pony-trekking. Worth watching is the annual Scottish Six Days Trial where an international field of Motor Cycle Trials riders compete over some of the roughest terrain in Britain around Fort William every May.

8. Scottish festivals

Everybody knows about the Edinburgh Festival and the Edinburgh Fringe, but T in the Park is the new Woodstock and there are cultural festivals throughout the year in many parts of the country.

9. Scottish hospitality

Welcome. Come awa ben! Wull ye no come back again?

10. The Scots Language

Stick in an learn mair!

Feel free to add another 90!

Pride might not always be a bad thing, but remember:

There's aye a muckle slippy stane at ilka bodie's door.

2 Anger

Then Yre come in with sturt and stryfe
His hand wes aye upoun his knyfe

(WILLIAM DUNBAR)

The word anger comes from Old Norse *angr*, which may
seem appropriate because the Vikings of the Sagas seem
to have suffered quite a lot from anger and roused quite
a bit in other people. But, in fact, the Old Norse word

angr actually meant sorrow or affliction. Now, there is food for thought!

There is a popular misconception that the Scots are argumentative and aggressive. Not at all. We may have inherited a greater proportion of red-heads than most nations from the Vikings but we are a very peaceful people. Nevertheless, just now and again, historical events have awakened in us a sense of injustice and we have been roused to anger so, if you feel the need to have strong words with someone, Scots has a few choice words to offer.

Anger – in Scots this can still mean a cause of anger, grief or vexation, a sense that is now obsolete in English but which harks back to the original Old Norse meaning of the word. In one of the most famous passages from his long narrative poem, *The Bruce* (1375), John Barbour writes that *Fredome is a noble thing;* he goes on to explain:

> *Na, he that ay has levyt fre*
> *May nocht knaw weill the propyrte,*
> *The angyr na the wrechyt dome*

That is couplyt to foule thyrldome,
Bot gyff that he had assayit it.
Than all perquer he suld it wyt
And suld think fredome mar to prys
Than all the gold in warld that is.

[No, he that has always lived free
May not know well the attribute,
The sorrow nor the wretched sentence
That is coupled to foul slavery.
Unless he had tried it.
Then fully by heart he should know it
And should think freedom more to be valued
Than all the gold that is in the world.]

Argie-bargie – argument.

Blaw-bye – a passing shower of rain; a quick outburst of anger.

Brulyie – commotion, quarrel.

Bunnet – hat, cap. *Tae dae yer bunnet* is to fly into a rage or make a fuss as in:

Whit is she daein her bunnet aboot noo?

Cangle – dispute.

A guid high fence micht prevent mony a cangle atween neighbours.

Carfuffle – dirturbance; disagreement. This can be quite trivial, a bit of a fuss, or a serious **stushie**.

Carnaptious – irritable. This is the ideal word for grumpy old men.

Cattiewurrie – a violent dispute. Claws and teeth may be engaged.

Collieshangie – a noisy dispute; an uproar.

Contermacious – argumentative.

Cool – *tae lat him cool in the skin he het in* is to let him calm down after a fit of anger.

Dirdum – retribution; a blow.

Dunt – a blow; to strike. The cat wakens me in the morning with a dunt from her nose, but a dunt could equally well refer to a damaging impact.

Flyte – scold; quarrel; insult; use abusive language. Flyting can describe anything from a serious breach of the peace to a mild rebuke. The lesser end of the flyting scale is seen in *Popular Opinions Or A Picture of Real Life* (1812):

> *We ane anither's toits now ken sae weel, Though whiles we flyte, we seldom anger feel.*

[We now know each other's foibles so well that although we sometimes exchange disapproving words, we seldom feel anger.]

Forflutten – severely scolded, having suffered a vituperative flyting.

Gie daggers – to look at in an aggressive way. An accused, when asked in court by the Procurator Fiscal why she 'shouted, swore and committed a breach of the peace', pointed at the complainant and declared:

She gied ma dug daggers!

Heckle – An Old English word for the instrument used to straighten flax gave us a verb, to heckle, with the sense 'to speak sharply and reprovingly (to), to give (someone) a dressing-down, to scold severely'. Heckling is much older in Scots than in English and was often used of the process of questioning parliamentary candidates. An English parliamentary candidate contesting a Scottish seat was upbraided by a voter for being English. The candidate replied "Indeed, my man, I am an Englishman. I was born and Englishman and I hope to die an

Englishman." "Michty me!" said the Scottish voter, "Hiv ye nae ambeetion?"

Now heckling is to be heard in comedy venues where Scots audiences have raised heckling to an art form. Heckling can also mean teasing or even provoking to anger.

Ire – Sir Gilbert Hay in the *Buke of the Law of Armys* (1456) writes of

The unresonable passiouns of ire.

Misca – to call someone bad names; denounce; slander.

Ootfa – a quarrel.

Pet – to take offence, sulk. *Tae hing the pettit lip* is to wear an injured and offended expression.

Propugnacious – quarrelsome, disputatious, easily roused to anger. This word is only recorded in the writing

of John Galt but he seems to have had a fondness for it.
In *The Provost* (1822) he writes:

There were certain propugnacious spirits in
the volunteers' committee; and they urged and
persuaded the others

and in his *Ringan Gilhaize* (1823) we find

The mistress was of so propugnacious a temper,
that the poor man saw no better for't than to yield
obedience.

Galt did not entirely make the word up, though. The
Dictionary of the Scots Language cites a seventeenth-
century usage of *propugning* in the sense of defending
a thesis.

Sherrack, shirrick, shirragle, shirrang, shirrakie, shirraglie – contention, noisy squabble, rumpus.

Snash – impertinence.

Dinnae gie us ony o yer snash!

Stushie – a commotion; a brawl.

There wis sic a stushie A haed tae send for the polis.

Tene – anger; annoyance. It is interesting to note that many of the illustrative quotations for words associated with anger make it clear that they are being used about people who have lost their sense of proportion; in the *Testament of Cresseid* (c.1500), Robert Henryson writes of

Mars the god of ire . . . but [without] *temperance in tene.*

Threap – assert persistently. This can be used positively or it can be akin to nagging.

Tulyie, tulzie – a brawl; to squabble. This is one of a small number of words which retain a trace of the old letter *yogh*, which was written like a *z* with a tail and hence appeared as *z* in print. It is actually pronounced like the *y* in *yes*, except where it has disappeared altogether. So the first spelling given here reflects the pronunciation better (tooley). Never trust a *z* in a Scottish surname such as *Menzies* or place-name such as *Culzean*.

Wrath – There are many Older Scots examples of wrath where there is a strong sense of excess and intemperance, perhaps leading to loss of judgement. A good example is from Sir Gilbert Hay's *Buik of King Alexander* (c.1460):

> *For wrathe and tene I woxe nere wode* [mad].

A saner and wholly justifiable emotion is harboured by the wife of Tam o' Shanter in Robert Burns' poem, as she awaits her errant husband,

> *Gatherin her brows like gatherin storm, Nursin her wrath tae keep it warm.*

Wuid – mad. In 1816, Sir Walter Scott linked two deadly sins in *Old Mortality*:

Pride and anger hae driven him clean wud.

A. Henderson's collection of *A Few Rare Proverbs* (1832) gives the self-evident advice:

Ne'er put a sword in a wud man's hand.

In his *Etymological Dictionary of the Scottish Language* (1825) John Jamieson glosses a gruesome saying:

Ye haud a stick in the wod man's e'e, i.e. you continue to provoke one already enraged.

An exercise for the foolhardy

To cause any carnaptious person to become wuid with anger, try building your own insult by selecting combinations of words from the template below:

YOU ARE A

bowfin, clarty, manky, mingin, honkin,
[Dirty and smelly]
lowpin, mawkit, lousy, scabby
[bug-infested]
gameramus, gowk, numpty, nyaff, tube, sodie-heid,
diddy [fool]

AND I AM GONNAE GIE YE

An Aberdeen sweetie [painful flick on the head
with the thumb]

A Glasgow kiss [head butt]

a *blatter, bluffert, chap, claucht, cloot, clour, crunt,*
dicht, dirdum, dunt, doosht, dunch, dunt, fornacket,
glent, gowf, ramiegeister, skelp, skite, swack, yowff
[blow, buffet, knock etc. – for the force of the blow,
be guided by the sound of the word].

The following phrases might also be useful:

It wisnae me.

Help! Murther! Polis!

Righteous anger

Alexander Arbuthnot, writing in the fifteenth century, sees a positive side to ire:

Feirsness and yre is callit kene curage.

[Fierceness and ire are called resolute courage].

The Scots are well known for their courage. The Scottish Regiments have a long and glorious history. Scots have fought in defence of freedom all over the world. Righteous Scottish ministers have called down the wrath of God upon Scottish sinners Sunday after Sunday, hopefully of that variety described by Gilbert of the Hay (1456):

ire in pitee, merci and grace.

Sometimes, a bit of ire can stir up some **smeddum** (see chapter on Sloth).

A million things for Scots to be angry about:

Midgies

You can smack them and whack them; in vain you'll
    attack them,
They know every move that you make;
If you manage to kill yin, another half million
Are ready tae come tae the wake!

(ANON.)

3 Envy

Nixt in the Dance followit Invy
Fild full of feid and fellony

(WILLIAM DUNBAR)

The sin of envy . . . as a soure-leavened vessel,
turneth all things put into it unto sournesse;

(DAVID DICKSON A Brief Explication of the Psalms,
3 vols, c.1652)

Envy, or in Older Scots invy, is defined in *A Dictionary the Older Scottish Tongue* as 'rancour or mortification at another's advantages; malice, animosity, or hostility arising from this or other causes'. It seems to have a claim to being the root of all evil (although this distinction is usually claimed by Avarice) because, as John Gau points out in *The Richt Vay to the Kingdom of Heuine* (1533), it was the besetting sin of

> The Dewil throww quhais inwi deid com in the wardil

> [The Devil through whose envy death came into the world].

A further early example of envy is described in a poem from 1570 in the Scottish Text Society's collection of *Satirical Poems of the Time of the Reformation*:

> This mortall feid [feud], this haitrent and inuie, Did first begin . . . Betuix twa brether, Cain and Abell.

A former source of much political tension throughout the history of Scotland has been the relationship between the Scots and the English, whom the Scots sometimes refer to as the *Auld Enemy*. John Leslie in *The Historie of Scotland*, translated in 1596 by James Dalrymple, writes about the late fourteenth century:

> *Efter this was lang peace betuein Scotl. and*
> *Ingland, an ald invie nochttheles, was ay seine*
> *betuein thame;*

and then he goes on to describe a brawl between a Scots gentleman and an Englishman on London Bridge. The Scot won. Those still harbouring envious and antagonistic thoughts are summed up in one of R. Wilson's poems (1822):

> *They frine an' fret at ithers' guid; Curs'd envy rots*
> *their vera bluid.*

Under those circumstances, one does not know whether to pity or condemn Aunt Kate:

> *My aunty Kate sits at her wheel, And sair she*
> *lightlies me; But weel ken I it's a' envy, For ne'er a*
> *jo* [sweetheart] *has she.*

(The Lark, A Select Collection of the Most Celebrated and
Newest Songs 1765)

There's very little envy in Scottish hearts, of course, but here are a few examples.

Ayst – is a Caithness word meaning to desire eagerly, to envy. This is at the less discreditable end of the Envy spectrum. Indeed, it may be seen as a spur to getting on in the world as this proverb from Caithness, recorded by John Mowat in 1916, suggests:

Em 'at 'ill ayest 'e silk goon will get 'e sleeve o't

[People with an ambition will get at least part of their aim].

There is a fine line between desire and envy and indeed some older uses of envy in Scots are more akin to the sense of the French *avoir envie*. The same folk-lorist is quoted in Alfred and Amy Johnston's *Old-Lore Miscellany* describing protection against envious people who would seek to take away your luck:

> Before he was allowed to start, the horses and
> plough had to be blessed and sprinkled with
> the oatmeal and salt which she carried in her
> apron, because she said the folk will be
> "aystin" me.

Ill-will – used as a verb, can mean to envy, as in E. C. Smith's *Mang Howes* (1925):

> The flichterin burdies daibbelt an dookeet; an
> A fair ill-wulled thum o ther plowtereen an ther
> swattereen.

> [The fluttering birds dabbled and ducked and I
> thoroughly envied them their messing about and
> splashing.]

Invy – envy. The job of a lexicographer is not to decide how a word ought to be used but to look at how a word has been used and to try to work out definitions from what people actually say and write. So, when we come across a quotation like this, we are well pleased:

I haue synnit in the . . . syn of invy beand evill
content . . . of the prosperite of other personis;
(JOHN IRLAND *Of Penance and Confession* c.1490)

King James VI of Scotland, later James I of England, comfortingly counsels in his *Essays of a Prentise in the Divine Art of Poesie* (1585):

Lose not heart, though pale inuye Bark at thy praise.

We also find invy used as a verb. In John Bellenden's translation of Boece's *The Chronicles of Scotland* (1531) the English King, Edward, is clearly up to no good towards the Scottish hero when he decides to

send his ambassatouris to the . . . men quhilkis
[who] *invyit Wallace mais.*

Invyful – full of malice, envious. Beware of
   Sweete sleeked lippes, false malicious inuyfull harts.
   (Robert Rollock *Lectures upon the First and Second Epistles of
                                 Paul to the Thessalonians* 1606)

Upeat – to eat up, to gall, to vex with envy or chagrin,
most often found in the form upeaten, is a useful verb to
show the destructive effects of envy on the sinner.

Closely related to the sin of envy is the sin of avarice
or greed. As may often be observed, the one begets the
other.

4 Greed

Nixt him in dans come Cuvatyce,
Rute of all evill and grund of vyce,
That nevir cowed be content.

(William Dunbar)

It is has often been said that the Scots are mean. The Scots
themselves have been known to attribute a mean streak

to the Aberdonians. Such stereotyping is never entirely justified and while some Scots may indeed be mean, most are just canny with money and a few are downright generous. Don't forget that the great philanthropist Andrew Carnegie was a Scot and all Scots are raised with the proverb

Ye canna tak it wi' ye.

While avarice is a major sin, to the Scots wastefulness is a worse one. For generations, the Scots existed in a fragile economy and thrift was one of the greatest housewifely virtues. This, coupled to a natural instinct for hospitality, provides another example of the Caledonian **antisyzygy** (see chapter on Pride).

So how have the Scots viewed generosity and parsimony in the past? Again, we can let the words speak for themselves.

Avarice – there is no doubt that avarice is seen as a black sin. A number of early quotations, like this one from Gilbert Hay's 1456 *Buke of the Law of Armys*, associate it with the very mouth of hell:

> *For he fell of the hevin, that is the haly kirk, in the mouth of the pitt of hell, that is avarice.*

John Knox did not approve of avarice (he did not approve of anything much) and railed against sin:

> *Especiallie avarice . . . excesse, ryotouse chear, banketting* [banquetting]*, immoderat dansing, and hurdome* [whoredom]*.*

A bizarre reference to avarice comes from Samuel Colvil, who claims that it makes people do rather odd things:

> *Avarice makes them . . . Keep rinded* [clarified] *butter in charter chests*
>> (*The Whigs Supplication, or, The Scots Hudibras* 1681)

Another curious reference to avarice comes in a document dated 1616, produced in evidence against a certain Thomas Ross. This Thomas Ross recommended that

all scottismen aucht to be throwin furthe and
expellit out of the court of England.

Why? He claimed that Saint Jerome, Augustine and
Strabo wrote that the Scots were cannibals and says
as yit the flesche whilk the ancient Scottis
swallowed stikis in the jawis and teith of the
courtioures quhairby thay ar provoikit to suche ane
insatiable avarice and intollerable pryde.

It seems that the Scottish courtiers who accompanied the
king to London were pretty unpopular! James's Scottish
judges recommended that Ross be hanged at the market
cross of Edinburgh and his head be fixed to one of the
gates

Canny – frugal, sparing, cautious. *Ca canny* means
'be careful'. It is our reputation for canniness that
inspires trust in the Scot's ability to handle money
wisely.

Fish guts – the phrase
> *Keep yer ain fish guts for yer ain sea maws*
> [seagulls] means that charity begins at home.

Fouthie – prosperous. A *fouth* is a fullness or abundance.

Gair – sharp; keen; greedy, covetous. Robert Tannahill in a poem of 1807 derides worldliness:
> *Thy Mither's gair an' set upon the warl,*
> *It's Muirland's gear that gars her like the carl.*

But John Galt takes a very balanced view in *Sir Andrew Wylie* (1822):
> *He's a wee gair, I aloo; but the liberal man's the*
> *beggar's brother*

and James Nicholson in *Idylls o'Hame* (1870) expresses a wholly approving attitude:
> *We never wantit, wife, For ye were aye sae gair.*

Of course, even a virtue can be taken to extremes, as
William Brockie laments in *The Confessional* (1876):

*An' yet she grudges me my meat . . . What does ane
live for but to eat? This gairness is a perfect staw*
[excess – probably used ironically, as a staw is
usually caused by a surfeit of food. See **Sta** under
Gluttony].

And, as is so often the case with ill-gotten gains, there is
no long-term benefit because, proverbially,

Gair-gathered siller Will no haud thegither.

Glamshach – greedy, grasping.

Gled – kite. This bird of prey is frequently modified
by the adjective greedy by such writers as James Hogg
(1832):

The greedy gleds and gairly fowls.

A chilling instance comes from Gavin Douglas's *Aeneid*
(1513):

The gredy gled . . . wachand the chiknys lyte, Thar deth mannasand [menacing]

and it is a wonder that the gled in the *Wyf of Auchtermuchty* ever got airborne again:

By thair cumis the gredy gled, And likkit vp fyve [goslings].

Greed – Synonymous with avarice or covetousness, greed is an interesting word because of its unusual origins. Greedy, the adjective, comes from Old English *grædig* and the noun greed is formed by removing the suffix. This is a backformation; usually adjectives are formed by adding a –y suffix to the noun, but this is working in the opposite direction. This seems to have happened earlier in Scots than in English because we have examples in *A Dictionary of the Older Scottish Tongue* dating from 1584, but the first citation in the *Oxford English Dictionary* is from 1609 – and even that is from a Scottish writer, Simion Grahame. So we can deduce that this is one of the many words which English has borrowed from Scots.

Grippie – tight-fisted; a mean person. A much-used word and, as this quotation from John Galt's *The Provost* (1822) shows, grippiness was sometimes more of a necessity than a sin:

Standing now clear and free of the world, I had less incitement to be so grippy.

Perhaps a grudging admiration may lurk behind J. Ballantyne's remark in *The Miller of Deanhaugh* (1844) that

auld grippy gets his work completed for half its value.

The same may be said of the fellow in Thomas Logan's poem (1871):

A shrewd pawkie carle, but grippy a wee,
Yet no a bad mortal when in a guid key.

Look closely at Effie's marriage qualifications – she might be ugly, but she certainly could hang onto the halfpennies:

> *Folk wondered at his takin' Effie, wha was a*
> *roch-lookin', ill-faured body, but gruppy wi'*
> *bawbees*

(William Blair Kildermoch 1910)

Gripple – this obsolete variation of grippie provides a 'dog in the manger' sentiment from Sir Walter Scott's *Marmion* (1808):

> *While gripple owners still refuse*
> *To others what they cannot use.*

Grub – to grasp (at money) in a mean or parsimonious manner.

> *I'm but ane humble dusty miller,*
> *No unco fond of grubbing siller*

(John MacTaggart The Scottish Gallovidian Encyclopedia)

Hame-drauchtit – selfish.

Huidpyk, hoodpik – a miser. An obsolete word but one used to great effect by William Dunbar:
> *Sum gevis to litill full wretchitly, That . . . for a huidpyk haldin is he.*

It makes a splendid insult in:
> *Hudpykis, hurdaris* [hoarders, especially of stolen goods], *and gadderaris* [gatherers];

Inhaudin – stingy.

Ken – know. *Tae ken the richt side o a bawbee* [halfpenny] is to be good at getting value for money.

Lang-nebbit – looking out for one's own advantage.

Largesse – generosity is the antidote to greed and walks the middle way. Sir Gilbert Hay, something of an authority on vices and virtues, praises largesse in *The Buke of Knychthede and The Buke of the Governaunce of Princis* (1456):

> *Larges quhilk is the myddis betwix prodigalitee and avarice.*

Liberality – this seems to be a good thing, according to John of Ireland in his *Mirror of Wisdom* (c.1490):

> *Humilite aganis pryde, liberalite aganis covatice.*

Lick-penny – a greedy, covetous person.

Meechie – stingy, tightfisted.

Nedynes, Nedines – parsimony, graspingness, avarice. Although it can mean 'in a state of need', it is often synonymous with covetousness in Older Scots texts. The *Thewis off Gudwomen* (c.1460) puts them together:

> *Gret couatice and gret nedynes*

and again the meaning is clear in Dalrymple's translation of John Leslie's *The Historie of Scotland* (1596):

He mekle [much] abhorit fra nedines and gredines, vices quhilkes [which] obscuir gretlie nobilitie.

Nosewise – keen-scented, perceptive, frequently used ironically. What has this to do with greed? You can smell greed a mile away!

I think you to nosvyse that has smellid your fathers avarice and falsety so far aff

(A quotation in the *Miscellany of the Scottish History Society* dating from 1630)

Prodigality – reckless extravagance. The Scots have no patience with this sort of thing. An entry from 1581 in the *Lennox Muniments* sums up our opinion of such wickedness:

Dame Elizabeth Dowglas . . . is idiot and prodigall having nowther tyme nor end of expenssis nor discretioun of hirself to rewll and governe hir landis . . . and gudis.

Puir – poor. *Tae mak a puir mou* [mouth] is to plead poverty as an excuse for meanness.

Rowp – public auction. This is what happens to the possessions of the unthrifty. It applies to all manner of property and some sales are quite specialised. An announcement in the *Edinburgh Gazette* of December 1700 announced,

> *There is to be a rouping of diverse sorts of Japan*
> *Work and other things for Adorning closetts*

and, in 2001, the *Press and Journal* advertised a roup at St Fergus public hall where

> *Wally* [china] *dogs and jewellery are among the*
> *many collectibles up for grabs.*

While the buyers might revel in the prospect of a bargain, in many instances the roup was an occasion of great suffering. Roups were often the result of poinding [pronounced 'pinding', seizure of a debtor's goods], and families in debt would be *rowpit oot* of their home or farm:

> Like pairtin' wi' yer flesh an' bluid It is tae see yer
> ain beasts roupit,

writes W. D. Cocker in his *Poems Scots and English* (1932).

Scrimp – mean, meagre; to economise, to be mean. One has to sympathise with James, the subject of John Brown's story *Jeems the Doorkeeper* (1864):

> Nature had finished off the rest of Jeems somewhat
> scrimply, as if she had run out of means.

More uplifting is a poem (1873) from Andrew Wanless:

> Folk, dinna be scrimp, 'twill gi'e life a relish,
> To be couthie and kind to the Poor o' the Parish.

Ticht – parsimonious. This literally means tight and is used as in English:

> he's ticht wi his money.

Wanthrift – the unforgivable sin of unthriftiness.

How to describe real misers

He wad rake hell for a saxpence. He wad flay a
louse for its skin
or, as it was put more forcefully by J. Service in *Dr.*
Duguid (1887):
He would have skinned a loose for the creesh
[grease] *o't and socht candy for the banes.*
He could peel an orange in his pooch [pocket].
He has deep pooches an short airms.
Ye'll have had yer tea. [Said to avoid offering
refreshment].

What canny Scots really think

A fuil an his siller is suin pairtit,
[A fool and his money are soon parted].

Tak care o the pence and the punds'll tak care o themsels.
Better hain weel not wark sair
[Better save well than get stressed out at work].
Yaise whit ye hae an ye'll nivvir want
Profits winna hide.
[Said disparagingly of someone who has been spending ostentatiously.]

Actions speak louder

The Scots rarely get into debt but, if they do, they pay their bills promptly because they know that
    short accoonts mak lang freens.

The Scots are in fact very generous and this has nothing to do with self interest, in spite of the proverb:
    A giein haun's aye gettin.
    [A giving hand is always getting].

Reminiscing about holidays 'doon the watter' to Rothesay, a Glasgow woman recalled how her family used to send their hamper on ahead with all the tinned food they would need for a fortnight:

> *Noo A'm talkin about a hamper nearly as big as this settee. Right? Because ye never knew when ye were gettin visitors and aw that*

(ROBINSON AND CRAWFORD Scotspeak 2001)

That is Scottish hospitality! Well, *it's nae loss whit a freen gets.*

5 Sloth

Syne sweirnes, at the secound bidding
Come lyk a sow out of a midding,
Ful slepy wes his grunyie [snout];

(WILLIAM DUNBAR)

This is not a sin that the Scots give in to. The work ethic is deeply ingrained and although there are occasional temptations and lapses, it is hard to find many examples of Scottish laziness. Robert Burns did express some reluctance in the lines

Up in the mornin's no for me,
Up in the mornin early;
When a' the hills are covered wisnaw,
I'm sure it's winter fairly.

but the Scots really do believe that

Early to bed, early to rise Makes a man healthy,
wealthy and wise.

In fact there are a large number of Scots sayings and admonitions against sloth, such as the one from the excellent *Consail and Teiching at the Vys* [wise] *Man gaif his Sone* sometime around 1460 to

Be besy euir and luf na sleuth.

More modern exhortations include:

Ae hour in the mornin is worth twa at nicht

[One hour in the morning is worth two at night].

Fit's deen's nae tae dae.
[What is done is not still to do].
Seener yokit seener deen.
[Sooner started, sooner done].
Sweirty is an enemy tae thrift.
[Laziness is an enemy to thrift].
A gangin fit's aye gettin.
[A going foot is always earning].

And one that definitely strikes a chord as the years fly past:
He that grieves maist grieves maist for wastit time.

See if you can recognise any Scots characteristics in the following.

Darg – a day's work; to work.

Dowf – dull; unresponsive, listless, inactive, melancholic. Scots are not impressed by an air of well-bred boredom, as we read in Sarah Tytler's *The Macdonald Lass* (1895):

*. . . her guests were compelled to come to the
conclusion that the fine lady had been attacked
by the vapours, so 'dowf' was she in her
stateliness.*

This man was in a bad way:

*Now grown mauchless, dowf and sweer aye To
look near his farm or wark*

(*Edinburgh Magazine* March 1795)

and it would have been an uphill job to flirt with
Strathfallan who, according to David Davidson's
Thoughts on the Seasons, (1789) was

as douf to love As an auld cabbage runt
[dried-up stalk].

Dozened, dozent – stupefied, dazed, impotent; dull,
stupid, heavy with sleep, often applied to those whose
faculties have deteriorated through age, drink, etc.

Early riser – a cynical proverb advises:

Get a name as an early riser and you can lie in your bed all day.

Early rising is not all it is cracked up to be:
The early bird catches the worm.
This proverb always makes me squirm;
The early worm that got up first
Unfortunately comes off worst.

(ANON.)

Fushionless – dull, flat, uninspired. The curate, John Halftext, in Sir Walter Scott's *Old Mortality* (1816) was unlikely to light any evangelical fires. His parishioner
will not wait upon the thowless, thriftless, fissenless ministry of that carnal man.

G. Outram uses the word in a very specific sense in *Legal and other Lyrics* (1874):
His houghs are gane, an' when nicht sets in, He's fusionless as a wether,

but it is a more general kind of marital inactivity that Alison Taylor castigates in *Bitter Bread* (1929):

Haven't I seen them working and slaving, poor
fules, from morn to nicht, just because they've
married some lazy fishionless creature?

A great word and ideal for people whose get up and go has got up and gone.

Idleset – idleness, laziness, reluctance to work. Idleset could be harmless relaxation, as in George Macdonald's *Sir Gibbie* (1879):

And here am I . . . sittin' here in idleseat, wi' my
fire, an' my brose, an' my bible,

but there is a slight sense of guilt at doing nothing. Robert Louis Stevenson's old lawyer in *Weir of Hermiston* (1897) has no patience with it:

Ye'll have to find some kind of a trade, for I'll never
support ye in idleset.

The same parental stricture applies in Lewis Grassic Gibbon's *Cloud Howe* (1933):

> *His father . . .would glunch and glare at every bit*
> *mouthful he saw his son eat– his hands had never*
> *held idleceit's bread.*

Idleset was not always a matter of choice, though. Unemployment was always a source of suffering and Alex. Murdoch points out the unfairness of circumstances in *Scotch Readings* (1886):

> *The bailies are no subject to idle-sets,*
> *like puir working-men.*

For those in work, the typical Scottish employer is embodied in *Swatches o' Hamespun* (1922):

> *Dubbies wis a driver an' keepit nae idleseet fowk*
> *aboot's place.*

Lazy – a lazy bed in Scots does not have a pillow and a duvet. Lazy beds are a method of planting potatoes (and other crops) on undug strips of soil and covering them with manure and sods from adjacent trenches.

Lurdan – is an archaic or literary word for lazy or for a lazy or loutish person. You've got to keep cracking the whip because

Let alane maks mony lurdanes.

(ALFRED HENDERSON *Proverbs* 1832).

Sloth was the sin which brought about the downfall of the Roman Empire, if John Learmont (1791) is to be believed:

Lurdane sloth O'ercoups them [Romans] *a'mang savage swarms O' Hun an' Goth.*

Maucht – bodily strength, might, power; mental ability. Pity the poor soul

sae dozen'd an' funi'd [benumbed] *wi' cauld, that she had neither farrach* [energy] *nor maughts.*

(R. FORBES *Journal from London to Portsmouth* 1755)

Tae mak a maucht is to make a move or effort (to do something), as in:

> *Ye see, it was just on the chap o' nine, and we were makin' maughts for oor bed, when I thocht I heard a bit stir i' the back-room*

(F. MACKENZIE Cruisie Sketches 1893)

Mauchtless – feeble, without strength or energy, limp, helpless; sluggish, lethargic, lackadaisical like the character in James Cock's *Simple Strains* (1824):

> *She's maughtless, doited, auld, an' crazy, An' tint [lost] a' spirit.*

Most of us can feel a bit mauchtless on Mondays.

Shilpit – emaciated, puny in growth, shrunken, pinched, with sharp starved-looking or drawn features. Some people are naturally built for sloth. You could hardly expect a day's work from a character in this condition. It is sometimes used in combination with nyaff (an insignificant person) for an intensive word picture:

a shilpit wee nyaff.

Sleep – a Scottish idiom that strikes English ears as strange is *to sleep in*. This simply means to oversleep. *To sleep in one's shoes* is to die a violent death as many did in George Muir's *The Clydeside Minstrelsy* (1816):

The dreary eighteenth day of June
Made mony a ane sleep in their shoon;
The British blood was split like dew Upon the field
of Waterloo.

Sleepin deid, or nearly dead through lack of sleep, used to be a common state for general practitioners in a one-man practice, as George Abel records in *Wylins fae my Wallet* (1916):

The doctor wisna sweer to road [reluctant to start travelling], *Tho' sleepin' deid wi' fag* [tiredness].

Sleuth – sloth. Slothful councillors are taken to task in the Inverness Records of 1652:

> *Thair hes beine great sleuth and slacknes in sum*
> *men anent thair coming to counsell dayes.*

Smeddum – this is the Scots' secret weapon against sloth. Our language has had its up and downs over the centuries, as have some of the words that it contains. Smeddum is one such word. It goes back to Anglo-Saxon *smeodoma*, meaning fine flour. In seventeenth-century Scotland, it referred to the finest particles of grain lost as dust in the grinding process and swept up as refuse or food for the miller's pigs. A century later, its meaning had been extended to any fine powder including a red precipitate of mercury, an insecticide known to Burns, who would have given the eponymous antihero of his poem *To a Louse*

> *a dose of fell* [powerful] *red smeddum.*

The notion of efficacy extended the meaning of the word to pith, strength or essence of a substance and so, in 1822, Galt describes good snuff as *sae brisk in the smeddum, so pleasant to the smell.*

Smeddum was applied figuratively to spirit, energy and courage. Burns wrote in 1787 of persons possessing *smeddum and rumblegumption.*

This is the sense in which Lewis Grassic Gibbon used it for the title of a short story.

Most revealingly, we find in the poems of James Mylne (1790) that

Afore he wrote, bauld Ramsay saw the smeddom o' our tongue decay.

Mylne, and Allan Ramsay, might have been surprised by the renewed smeddum in the Scots language today. As for the word itself, not only has smeddum ceased to be the sweepings of the mill floor but it is now one of the most valued qualities of the Scots character – grim and gritty energy and perseverance.

Sweir – lazy, slothful, disinclined to work, reluctant. Sir

James Balfour, of Pettindreich in *Practicks: or, a system of the more ancient Law of Scotland* (c.1575) puts a different slant on the fable of the grass-hopper who played all summer and in winter went to beg from his neighbour, the ant:

He that for swearnes and cauld wald not work in winter, sall thairfoir beg in the sommer time.

Of course there are certain tasks that cannot be undertaken if the weather is going to be bad and so

A sweir man's aye bodin' ill weather.

No doubt the shoemaker in J. C. Milne's *The Orra Loon* (1946) was just such a procrastinator:

The sweer souter's crookit tattie-dreels [potato rows] *Bleezin' wi' yalla skellach* [wild mustard].

Of course, on rare occasions, women have also been sweir, like Katie, the little sweir person in Allan Ramsay's rhyme (1736):

Ketty Sweerock frae where she sate, cries reik [pass] *me this and reik me that.*

And we read with some horror in the *Huntly Express* (11 February 1949) that:

> *Sweerty winna lat the wives rise tae mak' the brakfist.*

Sweir-drauchts, *sweir-tree* or *sweer-arse* is a game in which two people seated on the ground, facing one another with feet pressed against feet, hold hands or grasp a stick between them and tug so that one tries to pull the other to his feet. Charles Mackay in *Poetry and Humour* (1882) explains the indelicate nature of the last of these names:

> *a sport among Scottish children, in which two of them are seated on the ground, and, holding a stick between them, endeavour each of them to draw the other up from the sitting posture. The heaviest in the posterior wins the game.*

A sweir man's lade or *lift* is an extra load taken by a lazy person to avoid a double journey.

Sweir or sweirt can also mean reluctant without any

necessary implication of laziness. In fact, this quotation suggests that ministers may suffer from avarice rather than sloth when the question was raised in 1703 in the Presbytery in Orkney as to

> Whether it will make a Gospel Minister sweer to
> Preach if he wants [lacks] a Stipend?

Thowless – lacking energy or spirit, inactive, lethargic, listless, having little initiative or capability, ineffectual.

> The thowless loon daunners aboot like a knotless
> threid.

If there are, indeed, quite a lot of words for sloth in Scots, it may be because any evidence at all of this sin attracts immediate censure. It might seem like quite a harmless sin but it is well known that all it takes for evil to prevail is for good men to do nothing. Besides, as sins go, it is not a lot of fun. If you must lie around all day, which sin is preferable – sloth or lust?

6 Lust

Than lichery, that lathly cors,
Come berand lyk a bagit hors;
And Idilnes did him leid;
Thair wes with him ane vgly sort
And mony stynkand fowll tramort
That had in syn bene deid.

(WILLIAM DUNBAR)

[Then lechery, like a stallion, came bearing that
loathesome corpse and Idleness led him; there was

with him an ugly crowd and many a stinking half-
decayed corpse that had died in sin.]

One sense of lust is simply pleasure, enjoyment or delight,
as is obvious from the wholly innocent quotation from
The Foly of Fulys and the Thewis of Wysmen (c1460):
Vysdome . . . is . . . suetar als and of mare lust Than
erdly thing that man may gust

[Wisdom is sweeter and of more delight than any
earthly thing that man may taste].

But then the killjoys got their hands on it and gave it
additional senses of sensual or vicious pleasure, self-
indulgence, and intemperance, excess and sexual
promiscuity. So we find Gavin Douglas in the Prologue
to his *Aeneid* (1513) making the rather world-weary
comment about love:
Begynnyng with a fenyeit faynt plesance [false
feeble pleasure], *Continewit in lust and endyt with*
pennance

and John Knox roundly condemning those
> *Gevin to the filthy loostis of the fleshe.*

This is understandable, given the behaviour described by William Dunbar in his *Ballate Against Evil Women* where he likens a woman who is not choosy about her partner to a bitch on heat:
> *Quhone the biche is jolie and on rage Scho chesis not the grewhound in the hour, The foulest tyk* [scruffy dog] *quhill scho hir lust aswage.*

Women with such appetites would have been well pleased to meet these gentlemen:
> *The nychtis ar ouer schort to gentil men to commit there libedeneus lust*
>
> > (SIR DAVID LINDSAY *The Complaynte of Scotland* 1549)

unless the shortness of the night is not a reference to their prodigious staying power but a comment on the long hours of summer daylight in Northern latitudes. In

spite of their outwardly strait-laced attitude to sex, lust
or love, the Scots have never had any difficulty talking
about such things.

Auld fire – old flame.
> *An auld fire's suin kinnelt.*

Another version of this is listed in A. Henderson's
Proverbs (1832):
> *Cauld parritch is sooner het again than new anes*
> *made.*

Bidie-in – The *Daily Record* (20 February 1995) sums
this up neatly:
> *These days, couples are no longer introduced as*
> *husband-and-wife. This is the age of the 'bidey-*
> *in', the co-habitee, the 'partner', 'live-in lover' or*
> *'significant other'.*

Biting and scratching – There is a saying that
> *Biting and scratching is Scots folk's wooing.*

Certainly over-elaborate protestations of devotion are rare except in songs and poetry.

Cheep, cheeper – a wee kiss.

Click, cleek – a boyfriend; a girlfriend; a potentially amorous contact made during an evening out. This is exemplified by Robin Jenkins in *Fergus Lamont* (1979):

> "That big man in the kilt's awfully interested in
> Glaikit Mary," cried one of the girls. "Maybe he
> wants her for a click," said another.

See **Lumber**.

Cutty-stool – the stool of repentance. Thomas Newte explains in *Prospects and Observations, on a Tour in England and Scotland in 1785*:

> In most of the kirks there is a small gallery, fit to
> contain about half a dozen of persons, and painted
> black, placed in an elevated situation, near the
> roof of the church, which they call the cutty-stool,

and on which offenders against chastity are forced
to sit, during the time of divine service for three
Sundays.

(See **Trilapse**.)

Dance – *to dance the miller's reel, to dance the reel o'
Bogie, to dance the reel o stumpie* all mean to have sex:
   *Then she fell o'er, an' sae did I, An' danced the
   miller's reel, O.*

(*Merry Muses* 1796)

Dautie, dawty – darling.
   *Better an auld man's dautie than a young man's
   fool.*

Dawt – to pet, to caress.

Dunty – a mistress. A rather old-fashioned word and,
while it is quite forthright in its meaning, it sounds rather
more pleasant than some modern equivalents.

Edinburgh – The burgh records of 1589 record
that *this burgh is grittumlie defylet* [extremely
defiled] *with the vyce of fornicatioun.*

We can confirm that the capital of Scotland is now a
model of respectability.

Fud – the human posterior, the buttocks. The Fud Court
was the Kirk Session, as the court for dealing with cases
of fornication. George Muir writes in *The Clydesdale
Minstrelsy* (1816):
  Ance ilka [every] *month I do resort To hear what's
  done in the Fud Court.*

(See **Trilapse**, **Towdy**.) Fud-money, **taudy**-fee or buttock
mail, was the fine imposed by this court.

Heich-kiltit – high-kilted; immodest. John Service in
Dr. Duguid (1887) describes a
  conversation, though aye stopping short of

skulduddery itsel', was whyles, still and on, of a gey heich-kiltit kind.

Hochmagandy – This is defined in the *Dictionary of the Scots Language* as 'fornication', but hochmagandy sounds a lot more entertaining. John Lauderdale says in a 1796 poem:

Be not sair on hough-magandie, As it's a fit o' friendly passion, And vera muckle now in fashion.

But not everyone is so broadminded and so Robert Tannahill writes in 1805:

The priest convenes his scandal court, Tae ken what houghmagandie sport Has been gaun on within the parish,

no doubt with some kind of punishment in mind (see **Cutty-stool**, **Trilapse**).

Lumber – The *Edinburgh Evening News* (2 April 1999) provides a well-glossed illustration:

*When males spot a 'wee stoater' (good-looking
young woman) in the bar, they might be
inclined to try their 'patter' (witty chat) on her.
Impress her, and they might get a 'lumber'
(pick-up).*

If bars are not your thing, you could try the more
cultured option suggested by Anna Blair in *More Tea at
Miss Cranston's* (1991):

*the Art Galleries was a great place for girls and
fellas walkin', see if y'could get off. . .gettin' a
'lumber' or . . . gettin' a 'click' some of them used
to call it.*

Mairry – marry. In Scots you are mairrit *on* someone
rather than married *to* them.

Puddins – puddings, sausage-style preparations
of oatmeal (white puddins, mealy puddins) or blood
sausage (black pudding).

Puddins and paramours wald be hetlie handelit

[puddings and paramours should be dealt with
while hot.]

(JAMES CARMICHAEL *Collection of Proverbs* 1628)

Sculduddery – lewd behaviour, fornication,
unchastity. Edward Burt in *Letters from a Gentleman in
the North of Scotland* (c.1730) writes of people being
*brought before a presbytery, etc. to be questioned
for sculduddery, i.e. fornication or adultery.*

Dougal Graham writes (c.1779) of clerics who were a
little less intrusive:
*Then we gat anither sort o' gospel fouk they ca'd
curits they didna like sclududery wark, but said nae
meikle against it.*

Sir Walter Scott in *Heart of Midlothian* (1818) seems to
imply that the clergy's interest in the sculduddery of the
flock was less for the cure of their souls than for the
increase of their own coffers from the fines they could
raise in fud-money:

Officers, and constables, that can find out naething but a wee bit skulduddery for the benefit o' the Kirk-treasurer.

Smooch – snog, kiss and cuddle, especially during slow dances.

Smuirich – kiss.
Young Sandy kiss'd them ane an' a', An' Harry smoorich'd mair than twa

(ROBERT FORD *Hamespun Lays* 1878)

Store horse – In parts of Scotland the Co-operative Society shop is known as the store and, in the days when they used horses, these tended to be thick-set and unprepossessing beasts. Hence the expression often heard in Edinburgh:
Kiss you? A wid rather kiss the store horse.

Tanty-ranty, taunty-raunty – rumpy-pumpy.

Tocher – dowry. Make sure you read the small print:
> *Maidens' tochers and ministers' stipends are ay less
> than ca'd* [advertised].
> *A tocherless* [dowerless] *dame sits lang at hame.*

Towdy, taudy – the buttocks, the posterior. Towdy-fee was the fine imposed by the church courts for fornication, also known as buttock-mail.

Trilapse – a third fall into sin. Walter Steuart in *Collections concerning the Worship, etc. of the Church of Scotland* (1709) decrees:
> *Fornicators are to make profession of their
> repentance three several Sabbaths; who are guilty
> of a relapse therein, six Sabbaths; who are guilty of
> a trilapse, twenty-six Sabbaths.*

And if you think that's bad, the *Reliquiae Antiquae Scoticae*, edited by George Kinloch and Charles Baxter, gives from 1659 *Ane extract of the old laird of Mains his faults – viz.* **sextulaps** *in fornication.* Do we criticise or admire the old laird? The prize, however, goes to the sinner in Strathbogie who in 1653 was *Excommunicat for* **octolapse** *in fornication.*

Venerie – wanton behaviour, sexual excess. There should be a law against it! Aberdeen certainly thought so in 1497 when

> *It was statut and ordanit . . . that all licht weman be chargit and ordanit to decist fra thar vicis and syne of venerie, and al thair buthis and houssis skalit*

> [It was decreed and ordained . . . that all loose women be ordered and ordained to desist from their vices and sin of sexual excess and all their shops and houses dispersed].

Wad – wed. Marriage to strangers is not recommended:

> *Better wad ower the midden* [dung heap] *than ower the moor.*

Wench, winch – to court. This can mean anything from chaste romantic dalliance to brazen hochmagandie. At one end of the scale we read, in the *Herald* (5 June 2000):

> *I knew a couple in Govan who were winching*
> *for more than 30 years because they feared that*
> *marriage might destroy their good relationship.*

At the other end of the scale, the court reporter of the same newspaper writes (24 March 2000):

> *She told the court he wanted to go outside to*
> *"winch me". Prosecutor Norman Ritchie asked if*
> *that meant sex and she said: "Yes." She refused and*
> *went home.*

It is normally a matter of mutual consent and some tenderness, as experienced by the couple in Alan Spence's *Way to Go* (1999):

> *She turned and looked at me, amused, gave a wee*
> *chuckle, kissed me on the mouth hard and quick,*

and again, and we were kissing for real, lingering,
soft and moist and warm, me and Jeannie winching,
and I wanted it not to stop.

But most of us have experienced a moment of dawning,
horrified realisation:

"Oh," said Graeme, "I've winched a Bampot"
[a person given to unpredictable outbursts of stupid
or even violent behaviour].

(GORDON LEGGE *I Love Me (Who Do You Love?) 1994)*

7 Gluttony

Than the Fowll monster Glutteny
Off wame [stomach] *unsasiable and gredy,*
To dance he did him dres.
Him followit mony fowll drunckart [foul drunkards]
With can and collep, cop and quart,
[various drinking vessels]
In surfeit and excess.
Full mony a waistles wallydrag [slovenly fellow]

With wamis unweildable did furth wag
In creishe [fat] *that did incres.*

(WILLIAM DUNBAR)

There might be a very good excuse for waggling unwieldy wobbly bits in Scotland, a country of outstanding food and drink. There are the soft fruits such as Perthshire raspberries; tasty lean beef from our native Highland Cattle and succulent Aberdeen Angus steaks; rich cream and cheeses from the dairies of Ayrshire and Lanarkshire and wild salmon from the Spey, the Dee, the Tay, the Tweed and the other great salmon rivers. Arbroath Smokies, Finnan Haddock, Loch Fyne Kippers, Aberdeen Butteries, Dundee Marmalade and Forfar Bridies are just some of the stops on the gastronomic map of Scotland.

Eating

Belligut – a glutton; greedy. The *Stonehaven Journal* (13 June 1872) describes

a parcel o' bellygut rascals, wha kent o' naething
but livin' upon turkies an' port wine.

Creesh – fat, grease. While a creeshie person might
be corpulent or unctuous, creesh is often specifically
applied to the fat of fowls, as in the *Aberdeen Press and
Journal* of 21 March 1992:

Creesh was the lump of fat from the inside of a
hen; and when rubbed liberally on leather it made
a first-class water repellent.

Horse-creesh, the fat surrounding the entrails of a horse,
was rubbed in to ease sprains.

A different kind of creesh, but an equally useful
one, is described by J. Firth in the *Orkney and Shetland
Miscellancy* (1913):—

When wool was being prepared for a web a
mixture of whale-oil and tar melted together, and
called creesh, was sprinkled out of an old cruizie
lamp on the heap of wool laid on the floor.

According to A. Hislop's *The Proverbs of Scotland* (1870), *Butter's the king o' a' creesh* and the lubricating powers of butter are well attested; the 1527 *Accounts of the Treasurer of Scotland* show an entry *For Orkney buttir to creische the quhelis* (wheels). J. Kelly in *A Complete Collection of Scottish Proverbs* (1721) is scathing, unjustifiably claiming Orkney butter is

neither good to eat, nor to creich wool.

Creeshin someone's luif (greasing someone's palm) can imply payment for a service, or it may carry undertones of bribery.

A tasty dish creeshes the tongue or teeth. This was the sense used by Robert Henryson in his retelling of the Aesop fable in which the town mouse and the country mouse ate

A quhyt (white) candill out of a coffer stall, In steid of spyce to cresch thair teithis withall.

For all the practical uses of creesh, it is this substance which brings both mice and men to the sin of gluttony.

Who could resist the temptations that Allan Ramsay offers (1722)?

> *Beef, and Broe* [gravy], *and Gryce* [pork], *and Geese, And Pyes a' rinning o'er wi' Creesh.*

Finally, the concept of 'fat cats' is not unknown in Scotland as Roderick Watson claims in *The New Makars* (1991) edited by Tom Hubbard:

> *God'll shairly keep the heid yins* [top people]
> *Wrappit in creesh an peace at hame,*
> *Sin they never kent the dirl o needin.*

Fat – *A Dictionary of the Older Scottish Tongue* defines this adjective with the utmost delicacy:

> *Of persons or animals: More than ordinarily fleshy*

and illustrates it with an elegant simile from Andrew of Wyntoun's *Orygynale Cronykil of Scotland* (c.1420):

> *The carle* [fellow] *was fat as ony selch* [seal].

Gust, guste – taste, relish. The Scots always knew a good thing when they tasted it:

> *Claret wyne that is . . . delytable of hewe and gust*
>
> (SIR GILBERT HAY *Buke of the Governaunce of Princis* 1456)

Not only colour and taste, but also texture, are food for the senses:

> *This froit* [fruit] *. . . in guste, in twiching* [touching],
> *it has all maner of plesaunce*
>
> (JOHN OF IRELAND *The Meroure of Wyssdome* 1490)

To enjoy Scottish salmon at their most gustie, please note:

> *Thir* [these] *salmond, . . . eftir thair spawning,*
> *. . . hes sa warsche* [see **Wersh**] *gust, that thay ar*
> *unproffitable to eit*
>
> (*The Chronicles of Scotland*, compiled by HECTOR BOECE,
> translated by JOHN BELLENDEN 1531)

Hunger – a commonly used expression is *a hunger or a burst*, meaning 'a period of privation followed by a period of prosperity', 'a feast or a famine'. A picturesque illustration is found in the *Laird of Logan* (1854):

> *As for feasting, it's either a hunger or a burst wi' us;*
> *for, if I'm sent ae night to my bed wi' my stomach*
> *stuffed like a Yule haggis, maybe for a week after*
> *it will be as toom [empty] as my master's pouch*
> *[pocket].*

In many trades where income was uncertain, a hunger or a burst was familiar; although fishing was a hazardous occupation and catches fluctuated, J. G. Bertram tells us in *Harvest of Sea* (1865):

> *There is usually on the average of the year a*
> *steady income, the people seldom suffering from*
> *'a hunger and a burst' like weavers and other*
> *handicraftsmen.*

Hunger can also be used as a verb. A seemingly modern thought for the over-zealous slimmer comes from Patrick Walker's *Some Remarkable Passages of the Life and Death of Mr Alexander Peden* (1724):

Christ minds only to diet you, and not to hunger you.

Sadly, *diet* here simply means 'feed'! The actions of a belligut are enumerated by Dougal Graham (c.1779):

She's aye flyting on [scolding] *her lasses, hungers her servant lad, eats cocks and hens hersel, and gars the poor minister eat saut herrin.*

Hungert – underfed, starved. Like the two lucky rats in *An Old Wigtownshire Body's Fables frae the French* (1912):

Twa hungert Rats were gaun aboot an' fun' An egg baith guid an' fresh upon the grun'.

Parritch – porridge; oatmeal boiled in salted water, a staple of the Scottish diet. A perusal of these quotations shows that the opportunities for the sin of gluttony were pretty limited in Scotland for many years.

The 1795 *Statistical Account* for Moray confirms that

The diet of the labouring people here, and in
general, all through the Lowlands of the North of
Scotland, is porridge, made of oat meal, with milk
or beer, to breakfast.

Menu suggestions for the rest of the day come from the
Scots Magazine (December 1953):

It was parritch in the mornin, oatmeal fried in creesh
and tatties at dennertime, and parritch at nicht.

This might sound plain but it seems to have been good
enough for Burns in *The Cotter's Saturday Night* (1786):

But now the Supper crowns their simple board, The
halesome Porritch, chief of Scotia's food;

and the prospect of this meagre fare, according to William
Tennant in *Papistry Storm'd* (1827), was occasion for

Singin' and dringin' [loitering], *token clear That*
merry parridge-time was near.

Indeed, the results of even slight overindulgence were
quickly noticed:

I doot some o' ye hae taen ower mony whey porridge the day

(*Border Treasury* 1 August 1874)

Parritch (and soup) demonstrate a quirk of Scots grammar in that they are often used as if they were plural. Sir Walter Scott does this in Old Mortality (1816):

"They're gude parritch eneugh," said Mrs. Wilson, "if ye wad but take time to sup them".

Robert Louis Stevenson also does this in *Kidnapped* (1886):

They're fine, halesome food – they're grand food, parritch.

Something that is *as plain as parritch* is self-evident and obvious to all.

After a period of comparative luxury, it seems one always has to get *back to auld claes an' parritch*, or the humdrum workaday world of sober reality. You might even be so poor that you are *no able to buy saut* [salt] *tae yer parritch* which would mean that you were very poor indeed. Of course that may be because you are *no worth the saut tae yer parritch*, in which case you are a complete waste of space. Telling someone to *save yer breath tae cool yer parritch*, is a way of telling them to mind their own business and keep their mouths shut.

Sta, staw – a surfeit, a feeling of nausea, disgust or aversion caused by satiety; a jollification involving much eating of tit-bits. If you *tak a staw* at something you are disgusted by it, often as the result of an excess.

Wersh – this is a difficult word to pin down because some people perceive wershness as bitterness and others regard it as unpleasant blandness. Earlier uses seem to be more in line with wersh as a synonym for weak, feeble and lacking in flavour. Ramsay's *Proverbs* (1736) tells us that

A kiss and a drink of water is but a wersh disjune
[breakfast]'.

Quite a few of the quotations in the *Dictionary of the
Scots Language* refer to lack of salt. *As wersh as saltless
kail* is an apt simile to demonstrate this sense. Porridge
without salt is pretty wersh too. Jamieson illustrates
wersh in his 1825 dictionary with:

I dinna like them [porridge]; *they're unco werse;
gie me a wee pickle saut.*

Using the word figuratively and alliteratively, the
Transactions of the Hawick Archaeological Society
(1862) record that

*The minister had a weary warsle wi' a wersh
discourse*

and most students have sat through a wersh lecture or
two. Wersh weather is raw and damp. Even a kiss might
be wersh:

A kiss athoot a beard is like an egg athoot saut.

The later sense of bitter or sour does not appear until the early twentieth century and sour is clearly what is intended by Hugh McDiarmid in *Sangschaw* (1925):
Wersh is the vinegar.

Drinking

The Scots are an abstemious people but there is a minority who occasionally find
the maut abuin the meal
[the malt above the meal].

The rest of us can then sit soberly by and think up words to describe people in varying degrees of drunkenness. The *Herald* of 30 October 1993 noted:
An Englishman can be drunk but a Scot can be fou, smeekit, roarie, the worse o drink, blin fou, roarin fou, fou as a puggie, fou as a wulk, miraculous, pie-eyed, mortal, steamin, steamboats, mingin, fleein,

greetin fou, stottin, soople, spuin fou, drouthie, sappie.

Here are some of these and other useful words to describe drink and its undesirable outcomes in Scots.

Aquavite – aqua vitæ, whisky, 'water of life'. *The Historie of Scotland* by Johne Leslie, translated by James Dalrymple (1596), observes that

In this cuntrie thay lykwyse sell aqua vitae, quhilk [which] *heir in place of wine thay commonlie vse.*

The Laing Manuscript of 1658 mentions a mouthwatering occasion:

A teastting of our wastland hearrings
[a tasting of our westland herrings]
and Glasgowe acquavytie to disgestt them.

But there were abuses such as the

Frequent prophanation of the Lordes day in this paroich by aquavitey bearers, disapproved of by the Dingwall Presbytery in 1649.

Blaand, blaund – whey mixed with water, a popular drink in Shetland. Jessie Saxby in *The Old Lore Miscellany* (1914) suggests it may even have restorative powers:

> *Blaund, whey of buttermilk. The whey is allowed to reach the fermenting, sparkling stage. Beyond that it becomes flat and vinegary. 'Soor blaund' is a delicious and quenching drink, and used to be in every cottage for common use. It is what fashionable doctors recommend for consumptives under the name of the 'sour whey cure.'*

The trows are particularly fond of blaand and wise householders leave a cup for these supernatural inhabitants of the Northern Isles.

Bleezed, bleezin – very drunk. Jamieson, in his Scots dictionary of 1808, defines bleezed as the state of one on whom intoxicating liquor begins to operate.

William Alexander gives a slightly later example of bleezin in *Johnny Gibb* (1871):

> *That vera nicht he came hame fae the dominie's*
> *bleezin' – he's takin' sair to the drink.*

Bleezin'-fou is uproariously drunk.

Bluitered, blootered – very drunk.

Drouth – thirst, lack of moisture. A good drouth is welcome on washday, because it means that atmospheric conditions are ideal for drying clothes outside. A drinker's drouth is a symptom of dehydration, caused by an excess of alcohol the night before. If you are drouthy, you are in need of a drink like Souter Johnny, Tam o' Shanter's *ancient trusted drouthy crony* in the Burns poem (1791).

Fleein – violently excited by rage or drink.

Fou – full. This is the usual Scots word for 'full' in

any context, but it does often mean 'full of drink'. It is possible to be *bitch, blin, greetin* [weeping], *roarin, spuin* [vomiting], *stottin* [bouncing] or *tumblin fou*, and taken to extremes one might become *fou as a buckie* [winkle], *fou as a whulk, fou as a piper, fou as a puggie* [monkey], *fou as the Baltic, fou as the ee o' a pick* [the ee is the eye-shaped hole in the head of the pick into which the handle is inserted] or *fou as a fiddler's bitch*. Or if you are wise, you can stop when you are just *fouish*.

These states can bring about such alarmingly foolish acts as that described by John Service in *Dr. Duguid* (1887):

> *Being as fou's a biled wulk* [boiled whelk], *he put three chairges in the gun, stapping them doon till it was primed to the muzzle, juist like himsel'.*

Roarin fou was a regular state for Tam o' Shanter. His wife complains:

> *ev'ry naig was ca'd a shoe on, The smith and thee gat roaring fou on.*

Glamourie – a bewitched state.

> *Et Ne'erday some maun aye be fou gin morn*
> *for glaikit lauchter* [daft laughter] *or for gytit greetin*
>   [foolish weeping];
> *a glamourie bides in yill* [ale] *an usquebae.*
>
> (WILLIAM NEILL *Making Tracks* 1988)

Hauf – a half-gill of whisky. If you go into a pub and order a half, do not expect to be given a half pint of beer. Of course, you could hedge your bets and order a hauf an a hauf, in which case you get both and might feel very much at home in

> *an old-fashioned kind of place, all haufs and*
> *screwtaps and bunnets*
>
> (HERALD 6 June 1997)

Magnum bonum – a bottle containing two quarts of wine or spirits, or the contents thereof. A quotation from c.1755 commemorates a wine drinker:

> *His fondness for claret brought him the nickname*
> *of Dr Bonum Magnum.*

A wry contrast between the Episcopal church and the Presbyterian church is made in *The Bee* (March 1791):

> *In the time of episcopacy, the dean used to*
> *call boldly for a bottle of wine. Afterwards, the*
> *moderator whispered the maid to fetch a magnum*
> *bonum.*

The moderator should have been less coy, as his knowledge of Latin would have told him that a magnum bonum is 'a big good thing'.

Maut – malt The basis of ale or whisky, hence the drink itself. Ebenezer Picken, in a poem of 1788, expresses the wish:

> *Foul fa' the chiel'*
> [bad luck to the fellow]
> *wha thinks't a faut* [fault],
> *To meddle wi' the juice o' maut*

and indeed there are times when a celebratory drink is in order, such as when the aptly named *groanin maut,* is brewed to celebrate a birth. Robert Burns knew all about this! In *The Rantin Dog* he writes

> *O, wha will buy the groanin maut?. . . The rantin dog, the daddie o't!*

No doubt there were a few mornings after when he would have been moved to agree with James Stewart's request in his *Sketches of Scottish Character* (1857):

> *Then awa wi' your mautit potation, A waucht* [draught] *o' pure water for me.*

Mingin – smelly; stinking drunk.

Miraculous – It is hard to see how this could have become a slang term for drunk since there seems to be very little in the way of divine intervention involved.

Mortal – very, very drunk. An example comes from Alan Warner's novel *The Sopranos* (1999):

> *She was feeling bad cause she heard the next*

Saturday, he'd thumbed it the nine mile home
without a lift, mortal as a newt.

Pie-eyed – cross-eyed with drink.

Plottie – a hot beverage usually of toddy or punch
made with hot mulled wine and spices. We find this
comforting concoction in Sir Walter Scott's *St. Ronan's
Well* (1823):

Get us a jug of mulled wine – plottie, as you call it
. . . Your plottie is excellent, ever since I taught you
to mix the spices in the right proportion.

It was also being enjoyed in December of 1831,
according to the *Perthshire Advertiser*:

[He] *very considerately invited the party into a*
neighbour's house to get a 'plotty' and a merry
plotty they had, 'little waur than a wedding.'

It is a bit of an acquired taste and not universally liked;
Chambers' *Journal* (27 January 1906) describes

Rounds of beef, turkeys, and jeelies, washed down
by an abominable compound of port wine negus
called 'plottie'.

Reezie – giddy, light-headed, hilarious, especially as the result of drink. Chambers' *Edinburgh Journal* (1836) puts reezie in context:

If the ale be good . . . they begin to get cracky . . .
This second modicum brings them from cracky to
reezy; they are not fou, but just have plenty.

Refreshment – a euphemism for an aloholic drink.
He stopped for a wee refreshment on the way
home. Jist the wan.

Sappie – moist; sodden; well steeped in liquor – of things and people.

Screwtap – a bottle with a top which unscrews, traditionally containing beer; but more recently wine has started to appear in bottles which do not necessitate

the use of a corkscrew and, at dinner parties all round
Scotland, you can hear delighted cries of
   Ooh my favourite! Château Screwtap!

Sensation – a small quantity.
   *"Would you like a drink?" "Oh, jist the smallest
   sensation."*

To which my elderly mother has been known to add –
   " Weel maybe nae that small!"

Slocken – quench (of fire or thirst); slake. A poem of
1797 by Robert Buchanan proposes:
   Let's tak a slock'nin waught o' beer.

Thirst can be slockened with innocent liquids. The
Weekly Scotsman (6 August 1964) reports
   *There wasn't enough water available to slocken the
   drouth [thirst] of a moose [mouse],*

but if your companion expresses a desire for *a slockener,*

best head for the nearest pub and hope that he does not have the capacity referred to by Alexander Rodger in of a poem written before 1846:

What I've drunk might have slockened the sun.

Smeekit – smoked, inebriated.

Souple, soople – supple; limp; helpless (including through drink).

Stacher – to stagger, stumble about, totter, walk unsteadily. This may be the result of blameless youth, age or infirmity, but all too often it is attributable to drink. One such case is referred to by John Young in *Lochlomond Side* (1872):

When staucherin' fou He fell an' brack his leg.

Steamin – this word for drunk has an interesting origin. Until the mid-twentieth century in Scotland, alcoholic drink could only be served to the *bona fide* traveller. This led to people taking a trip down the Clyde on a steamboat and no one could deny that they were travelling. After a few drinks on board on the way there and a few more on the way back, they disembarked steamboats or steamin, so the story goes.

Swally – swallow; an alcoholic refreshment.
  Dae ye fancy a wee swally?

Usquebae – an earlier word for of whisky, now only in literary use. A source of courage to adventurers like Burns' Tam o' Shanter (1790):
  Wi' usquabae, we'll face the Devil!

A later imbiber was David Rorie's Auld Doctor 1920 who
  dined each day on the usquebae An' he washed it doon wi' haggis.

The word comes from Gaelic *uisge beatha* meaning 'water of life'.

Waucht – draught.
> We'll tak a richt [very] gude-willie [amicable]
> waucht For auld lang syne.

Whisky – a 1715 entry in *A Book of Scottish Pasquils* edited by James Maidment, warns
> Whiskie shall put our brains in rage

but Sir Robert Lockhart is more enthusiastic and his book on the *Whisky of Scotland* (1967) informs us:
> The blending of grain and malt whiskies, which is
> to-day a highly developed art, was not introduced
> until after 1860.

This could explain why Thomas Thomson wrote in 1849 that
> The whisky made by smugglers in Scotland is
> universally preferred by the inhabitants, and is
> purchased at a higher price, under the name of

Highland whisky. This is partly owing to its being made entirely from malt.

Today, there is no need to seek out contraband to enjoy a range of malts and blended whiskies to suit every palate.

Wine – a well-known soporific, a bringer of peace and sleep. This is evidenced in John Hamilton's *Ane Catholik and Facile Traictise* (1581):

The fume of the vyne montit on his harnes [brains], *sa that . . . he fell in sa sound a sleip.*

Of course a sufficient dose must be taken to achieve this effect or you get the unpleasant sensation disapproved of by Nicol Burne in his gripping yarn *The Disputation concerning the controversit Headdis of Religion hald in the realme of Scotland.* (1581). He recommends that

your merchandis sould nocht pas to Burdeouse [Bordeaux] *to bring hame vyne, becaus it makis monie of your headdis dissie.*

There has long been a friendly rivalry between Glasgow and Edinburgh and when it comes to wine, Glasgow scores points. Dalrymple's translation of Leslie's *The Historie of Scotland* (1596) praises Glasgow as

> the maist renoumed market in all the west . . .
> till Argyle, in the hilande Iles, and lykwyse to the
> outmest Iles in Irland it sendes baith vine and ale

but John Nicoll's *Diary of Public Transactions and other Occurrences* (1650–67) regrets that

> Much wynes sauld in Edinburgh wer corruptit and
> mixt, drawn over and kirned with milk, brinstone,
> and uther ingrediantis.

At least Mary Queen of Scots' mother knew to bring her cairry-oot with her:

> Your grace moun caus vevaris [food, provisions] *to*
> cum vyth the Franch men both of weyn and flour
> and uder nessesares for thar is lytell to geit in this
> cuntre
>
> (*The Scottish Correspondence of Mary of Lorraine* 1548–9)

Attendance at a birth seems to have been a convivial occasion since *the Foulis Account Book* contains a 1680 entry

> *For . . . claret wine to cummers and gossips*
> [godparents, close female companions]
> *when my wife was brought to bed.*

While the beneficial effects of red wine have often been noted, when it comes to white wine a rather poignant note is struck in an account of the execution of Lord Lovat (1747):

> *Upon which, the Warder ask'd his Lordship, what*
> *Wine he would please to have. Not white Wine,*
> *says he, unless you would have me go with the*
> *Skitter* [diarrhoea] *to the Block. For it seems white*
> *Wine generally gave him the Flux* [diarrhoea].

Yill – ale. To combine gluttony with avarice, follow this example from Sir Walter Scott's *Rob Roy* (1817):

> *I never gang to the yillhouse – that is unless ony*
> *neighbour was to gie me a pint.*

Two pieces of advice which make excellent sense when taken together are:

> *Yill-seasoned haivers* [foolish talk] *Are no worth a plack* [a coin of small value]

and

> *Yuill-sellers shouldna be story tellers.*

These come from John White's *Jottings* (1879) and John Service's *Dr. Duguid* (1887).

8 Mair, Maistlie Cantie Characteristics

Some of the quirks of the Scottish character are revealed in other words that we use about each other, which are not related either to the deadly sins or to cardinal virtues. After all, the Scots are a people of moderation in all things. Some of the best loved of these words are given below, some complimentary, some less so.

Braw – fine, splendid, illustrious.

Cantie – lively, cheerful, pleasant.

Couthie – agreeable, sociable, friendly, sympathetic; in comfortable circumstances.

Douce – sweet, pleasant. Sir Walter Scott in *Rob Roy* (1818) describes the old parliament which ceased in 1707:

> *When we had a Scots Parliament, . . . they sate dousely down and made laws for a hail country.*

Dour – determined, resolute, stern and hardy if you are referring to a Scot. Of non-Scots this means obstinate, stubborn, unwilling or sullen.

Gallus – This word has had an interesting history. It started off as fit for the gallows, villainous and rascally. It then moved up a little in the world to become tough, bold, perky, mischievous, impudent or high-spirited as in W. Hutcheson's *Chota Chants* (1937):

> *Next morning they werena sae gallus and frisky On finding the barrel was empty and light,*

or daring as in the *Scots Magazine* (April 1941):

> *"But I was gallus then," continued Tarn; "you know, game for anything",*

or wild and fun-loving, as a Perth informant implied in 1950:

> *She's a gallus lassie, aye fleein aroond wi the sodgers.*

The *Daily Mail* (17 February 1950) attempts a definition: *'Gallus,' that indeterminate but much-used expression in Glasgow, means hare-brained in a gay and flippant way.*

Glaikit – foolish, senseless. The *Transactions of the Hawick Archaeological Society* (1913) observes:

> *Town pipers seem to have been rather a glaikit lot, and by their indifference and neglect of duty, to have caused the municipal authorities much trouble.*

Heidit – This past participle of the verb heid, 'to furnish with a head', appears in a number of compounds suggesting mental confusion, such as **bee-heidit** and **peerie-heidit**. Joseph Tennant in *Jeannie Jaffray* (1909) extols the virtue of

> *a sensible gweed-leukin' lass . . . Nane o' yer fleein' bee-heidit craturs, withoot a grain o' soleedity.*

A peerie-heidit person is quite literally dizzy, because a peerie is a spinning top. Another more derogatory example is **mell-heidit**, having a head like a heavy wooden mallet. Current at least since the time of William Dunbar, it appears in the *Scots Magazine* of March 1806, to describe one of a pathetic trio:

> *Mell-headed Rab, wee limpin' Charlie, An' waddlin' Sam, the shauchlin' ferlie.*

None of these has anything to be **heich-heidit** about. A Buchan speaker (1929) issued the caveat:

> *She'll get the breeth o' her back yet for a' she's sae heich heidit,*

a colourful Scots rendering of 'Pride cometh before a fall'.

On the positive side, it is a great compliment to be described as **lang-heidit**. In her *Diary* (1815), Frances Burney d'Arblay describes *A woman that the Scotch would call long-headed; she was sagacious, penetrating, and gifted with strong humour* and the *Scots Magazine* (October 1823) uses the expression of Andrew Miller, *wha was anes reckoned among the langest-headed men in the parish, his advice sought by rich and poor round about.*

Paradoxically, heidit can also mean 'deprived of a head' as the past participle of heid meaning to behead. Hence a quotation on 1685 in W. Fraser's *Red Book of Grandtully* (1868) announces that *Argyll is to die on Tuesday nixt,*

whither headed or hanged I cannot yet tell.
It's enough to make you peerie-heidit.

Mensefu – well-mannered; restrained.

Perjink – means trim, neat, well turned out or smart in appearance. It is exemplified in W. D. Latto's *Tammas Bodkin* (1864), [She] *made me as clean an' perjink as a new preen*, and Neil Munro's *Daft Days* (1907), *In his clothing he was always trim and tidy, quite perjink, as hereabouts we say*. It can refer both to persons and things or places; the *Banffshire Journal* (9 February 1909) describes a house as *jist a perfect pictur' an' a'thing aboot the place that clean and perjink*. Alternatively, it can mean careful and precise as in *Lyon in Mourning* (1775):

> *But how came you not to observe the address I gave you literally and perjinkly?*

However, there is nothing good or bad but thinking

makes it so, and an excess of perjinkness can be less than attractive, tipping the meaning over into fussiness or priggishness. John Ruskin in *Praeterita* (1887) writes:

> *She had always what my mother called*
> *'perjinketty' ways, which made her typically an old*
> *maid in her later years*

and in Alison Fleming's *Christina Strang,* an overfastidious person is

> *That perjink ye'd think butter wadna melt in her moo.*

Perjink can also be used as a noun in the sense of a nicety or fussy detail. If you are *on your perjinks*, you are on your very best behaviour. John Galt, in *Sir Andrew Wylie* (1822), gives advice on

> *How to correct the press, and to put in the points,*
> *wi' the lave o' the wee perjinkities.*

Sonsie – lucky, friendly, good, honest, comely, sturdy. This adjective is most famously applied to the Haggis in the *Address to the Haggis* by Robert Burns:

Fair fa' [May good things happen to] *your honest, sonsie face, Great chieftain o' the puddin* [sausage] *race.*

Yet it is most often applied to young women of an attractive, healthy appearance. Hungert women are rarely sonsie.

Epilogue

I may be an old sinner but I am **proud** to be a Scot and a speaker of Scots. I get **angry** at people who undervalue this ancient and expressive language and I **envy** those Scots who also speak Gaelic. I cannot re-read the quotation about a tasting of herrings with aquavite as a digestif (see **Aquavite**) without an attack of mouth-watering **gluttony**. I was brought up to be grippie, in the best sense of the word, and if that makes me guilty of **avarice**, so be it, but, with the end of the book in sight, **sloth** prevents me from enumerating my other few failings and modesty forbids any mention of my many virtues.

We certainly have colourful and pithy words which allow us to criticise and sometimes laugh at ourselves. The quotations in this book may seem like a catalogue of excess of pleasure, foibles and weaknesses, folly and downright crimes, but they are the stuff that literature and newspaper reports are made of. As Mark Antony said of Caesar, *The good is oft interred with the bones* and flattering quotations are harder to find. Nevertheless, we Scots are much like anybody else, no better, no worse. As the old Scots saying would have it:

We are all Jock Tamson's bairns

or, as Robert Burns wrote:

For a' that, an' a' that,
It's comin' yet for a' that,
That Man to Man, the world o'er,
Shall brothers be for a' that.